Spanish
Piggyback® Songs

Written by Sonya Kranwinkel
Illustrated by Marion Ekberg
Chorded by Barbara Robinson

Totline® Publications
A Division of Frank Schaffer Publications, Inc.
Torrance, California

We wish to thank the following teachers, childcare workers, and parents for contributing some of the songs in this book: Nilda Medina, Brooklyn, NY; Sandy Minicozzi, Flanders, NJ; New Eton School Staff, Lomas de Chapultepec, Mexico; Aura Palacio, Memphis, TN; Vicki Shannon, Napton, MO; Sue St. John, Oregon, OH; Diane Thom, Maple Valley, WA; Sue Thomas, Kansas City, MO; and Jolynn Villena, Washington, PA.

Editorial Staff
  Managing Editor: Kathleen Cubley
  Contributing Editors: Susan Hodges, Wilma Illanes,
    Blanca Mikesell, Jean Warren
  Copy Editor: Kris Fulsaas
  Proofreader: Mae Rhodes
  Editorial Assistant: Kate Ffolliott

Design and Production Staff
  Art Manager: Uma Kukathas
  Book Design/Layout: Sarah Ness
  Cover Design: Brenda Mann Harrison
  Cover Illustration: Marion Ekberg
  Production Manager: JoAnna Brock

ISBN 1-57029-044-X

Library of Congress Catalog Card Number 94-78420
Printed in the United States of America
Published by: Totline® Publications
Editorial Office: P.O. Box 2250
              Everett, WA 98203
Business Office: 23740 Hawthorne Blvd.
              Torrance, CA 90505

20 19 18 17 16 15 14 13 12 11 10 9 8 7 6 5 4 3

Contents

Introduction

After working on this project for over two years, Totline® is proud to finally bring you *Spanish Piggyback® Songs*. Our goal was to develop a songbook for English-speaking parents and teachers who were interested in introducing simple Spanish words and phrases to their young children.

Included are some songs entirely in Spanish and some songs half in Spanish and half in English. For each song we have provided an English translation so you can quickly see if a certain song is appropriate for your immediate needs. Also accompanying each song is a Spanish pronunciation guide. These guides have been designed to be easily read as if they were English words. You will notice that some syllables are in capitals. This indicates that the syllable should be stressed. With a few exceptions, the songs have been written so that the accent in the song coincides with the stress in the Spanish word. For example, on page 7, "Fre-re JAC-que" coincides with "Kah-la-BAH-sa."

Young children love learning new words for familiar phrases and, as a rule, children under seven pick up languages very quickly and easily. So what better way to introduce your children to the lyrical language of Spanish than through song!

¡Bienvenidos a Spanish Piggyback Songs! ¡Que gocen!
(Welcome to Spanish Piggyback Songs! Enjoy!)

Autumn Leaves

Sung to: *Alouette*

C   G₇ C
Es otoño, it is autumn.

              G₇   C
Las hojas, the leaves begin to fall.

Falling, falling, falling,

Falling, falling, falling.
C   G₇ C
Oh, es otoño, it is autumn.

              G₇   C
Las hojas, the pretty leaves do fall.

C   G₇   C
Los colores, the autumn colors.

              G₇   C
Rojo, amarillo, red and yellow too.

Falling, falling, falling,

Falling, falling, falling.
C   G₇ C
Oh, es otoño, it is autumn.

              G₇   C
Las hojas, the pretty leaves do fall.

Sonya Kranwinkel

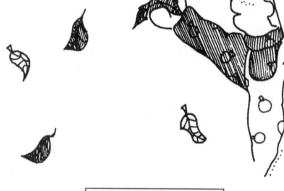

English Translation

It is autumn, it is autumn.
The leaves, the leaves begin to fall.
Falling, falling, falling,
Falling, falling, falling.
Oh, it is autumn, it is autumn.
The leaves, the pretty leaves do fall.

The colors, the autumn colors.
Red, yellow, red and yellow too.
Falling, falling, falling,
Falling, falling, falling.
Oh, it is autumn, it is autumn.
The leaves, the pretty leaves do fall.

Spanish Pronunciation

Es oh-TOAN-yo, it is autumn.
Loss OH-haws, the leaves begin to fall.
Falling, falling, falling,
Falling, falling, falling.
Oh, es oh-TOAN-yo, it is autumn.
Loss OH-haws, the pretty leaves do fall.

Loace co-LOAR-ace, the autumn colors.
ROE-ho, ah-maw-REE-yo, red and yellow too.
Falling, falling, falling,
Falling, falling, falling.
Oh, es oh-TOAN-yo, it is autumn.
Loss OH-haws, the pretty leaves do fall.

The Pumpkin

Sung to: *Frere Jacques*

c
Calabaza, calabaza,

Pumpkin, pumpkin.

Hacemos un pastel,

We'll make a pie,

A pumpkin pie.

A pumpkin pie.

Sonya Kranwinkel

English Translation

Pumpkin, pumpkin,
Pumpkin, pumpkin.
We'll make a pie,
We'll make a pie,
A pumpkin pie.
A pumpkin pie.

Spanish Pronunciation

Kah-la-BAH-sa, kah-la-BAH-sa,
Pumpkin, pumpkin.
Ahs-EM-ohs oon paust-ELL,
We'll make a pie,
A pumpkin pie.
A pumpkin pie.

Jack-O'-Lantern

Sung to: *Pop! Goes the Weasel*

D   A₇   D
Calabaza means pumpkin,
        A₇   D
Linterna means lantern,
           A₇   D   A₇   D
Linterna de calabaza means jack-o'-lantern.

Sonya Kranwinkel

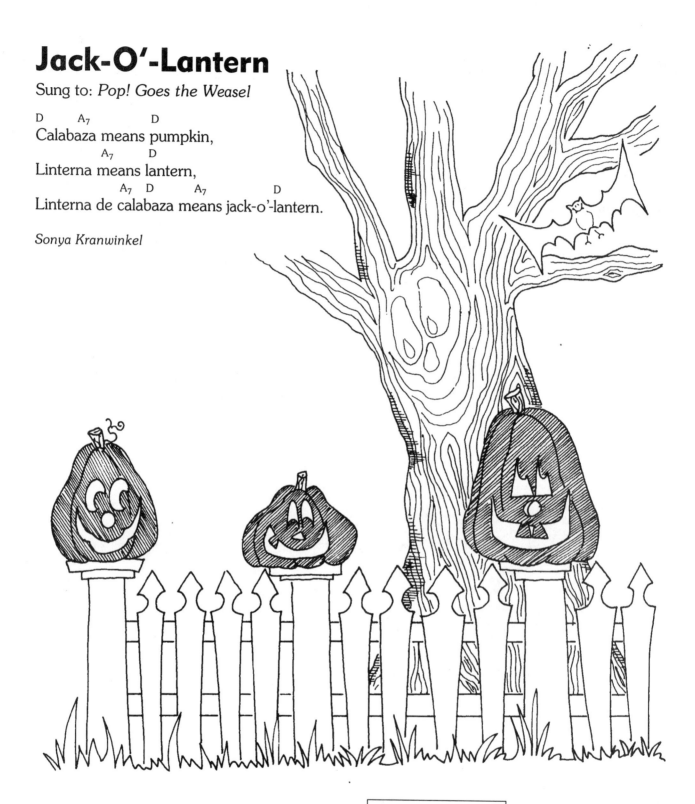

English Translation

Pumpkin means pumpkin,
Lantern means lantern,
Pumpkin lantern means jack-o'-lantern.

Spanish Pronunciation

Kah-la-BAH-sa means pumpkin,
Leen-TAIR-na means lantern,
Leen-TAIR-na day kah-la-BAH-sa means
   jack-o'-lantern.

Halloween Night

Sung to: *The Farmer in the Dell*

F
La noche de Halloween,

La noche de Halloween,

Salen los fantasmas.
C   F
¡Uhhh, uhhh, uhhh!

Additional verses: Salen los gatitos, miau,
miau, miau; Salen los payasos, ja, ja, ja, ja, ja.

Sonya Kranwinkel

English Translation

On Halloween night,
On Halloween night,
The ghosts come out.
Ooo, ooo, ooo!

Additional verses: The kittens come out,
meow, meow, meow; The clowns come out,
ha, ha, ha, ha, ha, ha.

Spanish Pronunciation

La NO-chay day Halloween,
La NO-chay day Halloween,
SAWL-en loace fawn-TAWS-moss.
Ooo, ooo, ooo!

Additional verses: SAWL-en loace gah-TEE-toes,
meow, meow, meow; SAWL-en loace pie-YAW-
soce, ha, ha, ha, ha, ha, ha.

Gobble, Gobble

Sung to: *Sing a Song of Sixpence*

C
La canción del pavo,
G7
Vamos a cantar.

We're going to sing
C
The turkey song.

Oigan al pavito,
G7
Cantando su canción:

¡Gobble, gobble, gobble, gobble,
C
Gobble, gobble, ooo!

Sonya Kranwinkel

English Translation

The song of the turkey,
We are going to sing.
We're going to sing
The turkey song.
Listen to the little turkey,
Singing his song:
Gobble, gobble, gobble, gobble,
Gobble, gobble, ooo!

Spanish Pronunciation

La kawn-see-OWN del PAUVE-oh,
VAH-moce ah kawn-TAR.
We're going to sing
The turkey song.
OY-gahn el pauve-EE-toe,
Kawn-TAHN-do soo kawn-see-OWN:
Gobble, gobble, gobble, gobble,
Gobble, gobble, ooo!

We Give Thanks

Sung to: *The Farmer in the Dell*

F
Damos las gracias,

Damos las gracias,

For food, and friends, and family,
    C₇   F
We give thanks.

F
Damos las gracias,

Damos las gracias,

Thanksgiving is the time to give
    C₇   F
Thanks to everyone.

Sonya Kranwinkel

English Translation

We give thanks,
We give thanks,
For food, and friends, and family,
We give thanks.

We give thanks,
We give thanks,
Thanksgiving is the time to give
Thanks to everyone.

Spanish Pronunciation

DA-moce loss GRAW-see-ahs,
DA-moce loss GRAW-see-ahs,
For food, and friends, and family,
We give thanks.

DA-moce loss GRAW-see-ahs,
DA-moce loss GRAW-see-ahs,
Thanksgiving is the time to give
Thanks to everyone.

Snowflakes Falling

Sung to: *For He's a Jolly Good Fellow*

    C   F   C
Empieza a caer la nieve,
    G₇   C
Empieza a caer la nieve,

Snowflakes all around,
G₇   C
Falling to the ground.

    C   F   C
Empieza a caer la nieve,
    G₇   C
Empieza a caer la nieve,

Snowflakes all around,
G₇   C
Making not a sound.

Sonya Kranwinkel

English Translation

The snow is starting to fall,
The snow is starting to fall,
Snowflakes all around,
Falling to the ground.

The snow is starting to fall,
The snow is starting to fall,
Snowflakes all around,
Making not a sound.

Spanish Pronunciation

Em-pee-ES-saw ah ky-AIR la nee-EV-vay,
Em-pee-ES-saw ah ky-AIR la nee-EV-vay,
Snowflakes all around,
Falling to the ground.

Em-pee-ES-saw ah ky-AIR la nee-EV-vay,
Em-pee-ES-saw ah ky-AIR la nee-EV-vay,
Snowflakes all around,
Making not a sound.

The Candles Shine

Sung to: *Alouette*

C
Las candelas,
G₇   C
Las candelas, ocho.

Eight candles,
G₇   C
All in a line.

C
Las candelas,
G₇   C
Brillan las candelas.

Shining candles,
G₇   C
It's Hanukkah time!

Sonya Kranwinkel

English Translation

The candles,
The candles, eight.
Eight candles,
All in a line.

The candles,
The candles shine.
Shining candles,
It's Hanukkah time!

Spanish Pronunciation

Loss kawn-DAY-loss,
Loss kawn-DAY-loss, OH-cho.
Eight candles,
All in a line.

Loss kawn-DAY-loss,
BREE-yahn loss kawn-DAY-loss,
Shining candles,
It's Hanukkah time!

Merry Christmas

Sung to: *The Farmer in the Dell*

F
Feliz Navidad,

Feliz Navidad,

Feliz Navidad,
C₇   F
A merry Christmas to you!

Sue St. John

English Translation

Merry Christmas,
Merry Christmas,
Merry Christmas,
A merry Christmas to you!

Spanish Pronunciation

Fay-LEESE Naw-vee-DAWD,
Fay-LEESE Naw-vee-DAWD,
Fay-LEESE Naw-vee-DAWD,
A merry Christmas to you!

Let's All Trim the Tree

Sung to: *I've Been Working on the Railroad*

G
Adornemos el arbolito,
C
Let's all trim the tree.

Hay que poner las luces,
    A₇   D
For everyone to see.
          G
El pinito bonito,
    C   B
The pretty pine tree.
C   G
Adornemos el arbolito,
       D   G
Let's all trim the tree.

Sonya Kranwinkel

English Translation

Let's trim the little tree,
Let's all trim the tree.
We need to put on the lights,
For everyone to see.
The pretty little pine tree,
The pretty pine tree.
Let's trim the little tree,
Let's all trim the tree.

Spanish Pronunciation

Ah-dore-NE-moce el ar-bo-LEE-toe,
Let's all trim the tree.
I kay po-NAIR loss LOO-saice,
For everyone to see.
El pee-NEE-toe bo-NEE-toe,
The pretty pine tree.
Ah-dore-NE-moce el ar-bo-LEE-toe,
Let's all trim the tree.

Jingle Bells

Sung to: *Jingle Bells*

F
Cascabel, cascabel,

Lindo cascabel.
C₇   F
Ringing notes of Christmastime,
G₇   C
Lindo cascabel.

F
Cascabel, cascabel,

Lindo cascabel.
C₇   F
Ringing notes of happiness,
C₇   F
Lindo cascabel.

Aura Palacio

English Translation

Jingle bells, jingle bells,
Pretty jingle bells.
Ringing notes of Christmastime,
Pretty jingle bells.

Jingle bells, jingle bells,
Pretty jingle bells.
Ringing notes of happiness,
Pretty jingle bells.

Spanish Pronunciation

Kaws-kah-BELL, kaws-kah-BELL,
LEEN-doe kaws-kah-BELL.
Ringing notes of Christmastime,
LEEN-doe kaws-kah-BELL.

Kaws-kah-BELL, kaws-kah-BELL,
LEEN-doe kaws-kah-BELL.
Ringing notes of happiness,
LEEN-doe kaws-kah-BELL.

New Year's Day

Sung to: *This Old Man*

C
¡Feliz año Nuevo!
F   G
Have a happy New Year's Day!
C
Clap your hands

And stamp your feet and say,
G₇   C   G₇   C
"Celebramos New Year's Day!"

Sonya Kranwinkel

English Translation

Happy
New Year!
Have a happy New Year's Day!
Clap your hands
And stamp your feet and say,
"We are celebrating New Year's Day!"

Spanish Pronunciation

Fay-LEESE AHN-yo
NWAY-vo!
Have a happy New Year's Day!
Clap your hands
And stamp your feet and say,
"Say-lay-BRAH-moce New Year's Day!"

Mother's Day

Sung to: *Frere Jacque*

C
Para mami,

Para mami,

Con amor,

Con amor,

Hice un regalo,

Hice un regalo,

Para ti,

Para ti.

Nilda Medina

English Translation	Spanish Pronunciation
For Mommy,	PA-rah mommy,
For Mommy,	PA-rah mommy,
With love,	Coan ah-MORE,
With love,	Coan ah-MORE,
I made a present,	EE-say oon ray-GAH-low,
I made a present,	EE-say oon ray-GAH-low,
For you,	PA-rah tee,
For you.	PA-rah tee.

The Little Rabbit

Sung to: *Down by the Station*

F
Conejito,
C   F
Little bunny rabbit,
     (Hold up two fingers.)

¿Dónde están sus huevos?
     (Shrug shoulders.)
C   F
Where are your eggs?

F
Conejito,
C   F
Easter is coming,

Hurry now
    C   F
And hide your eggs.
    (Put hands over eyes.)

Sonya Kranwinkel

English Translation

Little bunny rabbit,
Little bunny rabbit,
Where are your eggs?
Where are your eggs?

Little bunny rabbit,
Easter is coming,
Hurry now
And hide your eggs.

Spanish Pronunciation

Coan-nay-HEE-toe,
Little bunny rabbit,
DOAN-day ayy-STAWN soos HUAY-voce?
Where are your eggs?

Coan-nay-HEE-toe,
Easter is coming,
Hurry now
And hide your eggs.

Hidden Eggs

Sung to: *The Wheels on the Bus*

    F
Los huevos en la cesta

Están escondidos,
         C
Están escondidos,

Están escondidos.
    F
The eggs in the basket are hidden,
C   F
Hidden in the yard.

Additional verses: In the tree; Under the bush;
By the rock; etc.

Sonya Kranwinkel

English Translation

The eggs in the basket
Are hidden,
Are hidden,
Are hidden.
The eggs in the basket are hidden,
Hidden in the yard.

Spanish Pronunciation

Loace HUAY-voce ehn la SESS-ta
Ayy-STAWN es-coan-DEE-doce,
Ayy-STAWN es-coan-DEE-doce,
Ayy-STAWN es-coan-DEE-doce.
The eggs in the basket are hidden,
Hidden in the yard.

Pretty Yellow Chicks

Sung to: *Skip to My Lou*

C
Los pollitos amarillos,
G₇
Los pollitos amarillos,
C
Los pollitos amarillos,
G₇   C
Pretty yellow chicks.

C
Pío, pío, cheep, cheep, cheep,
G₇
Pío, pío, cheep, cheep, cheep,
C
Pío, pío, cheep, cheep, cheep,
G₇   C
Pío, pío, pío.

Sonya Kranwinkel

English Translation

The yellow chicks,
The yellow chicks,
The yellow chicks,
Pretty yellow chicks.

Cheep, cheep, cheep, cheep, cheep,
Cheep, cheep, cheep, cheep, cheep,
Cheep, cheep, cheep, cheep, cheep,
Cheep, cheep, cheep.

Spanish Pronunciation

Loace po-YEE-toce ah-maw-REE-yoce,
Loace po-YEE-toce ah-maw-REE-yoce,
Loace po-YEE-toce ah-maw-REE-yoce,
Pretty yellow chicks.

PEE-oh, PEE-oh, cheep, cheep, cheep,
PEE-oh, PEE-oh, cheep, cheep, cheep,
PEE-oh, PEE-oh, cheep, cheep, cheep,
PEE-oh, PEE-oh, PEE-oh.

Spring Flowers

Sung to: *I'm a Little Teapot*

C
La primavera,
F   C
In springtime,
G7   C   G7   C
Pretty flowers all around.

Rosas, margaritas,
F   C
Dientes de león,
        F   G7   C
Roses, daisies, and dandelions.

Sonya Kranwinkel

English Translation

The springtime,

In springtime,

Pretty flowers all around.

Roses, daisies,

Dandelions,

Roses, daisies, and dandelions.

Spanish Pronunciation

La pree-maw-VAIR-ra,

In springtime,

Pretty flowers all around.

ROE-saws, mar-gar-REE-taws,

Dee-ENT-tays day lee-OAN,

Roses, daisies, and dandelions.

Rain

Sung to: *Oh, Christmas Tree*

F
La lluvia, la lluvia,
B♭   C F
The rain is falling down.

La lluvia, la lluvia,
B♭   C   F
The rain helps things grow.
F   B♭
The corn, the beans, the flowers,
C   F
The grass and trees and bushes grow.

La lluvia, la lluvia,
B♭   C   F
The rain helps things grow.

Sonya Kranwinkel

English Translation

The rain, the rain,
The rain is falling down.
The rain, the rain,
The rain helps things grow.
The corn, the beans, the flowers,
The grass and trees and bushes grow.
The rain, the rain,
The rain helps things grow.

Spanish Pronunciation

La YOO-vee-ah, la YOO-vee-ah,
The rain is falling down.
La YOO-vee-ah, la YOO-vee-ah,
The rain helps things grow.
The corn, the beans, the flowers,
The grass and trees and bushes grow.
La YOO-vee-ah, la YOO-vee-ah,
The rain helps things grow.

Father's Day

Sung to: *Down by the Station*

F
Hoy es su día,
C   F
Querido Papito.

Quiero decirle,
C   F
De mi corazoncito,

Que yo le quiero,
C   F
Y le adoro.

¡Le doy un beso,
C   F
Y un abrazo!

Jolynn Villena

English Translation

Today is your day,
Dear Father.
I want to tell you,
From my little heart,
That I love you,
And adore you.
I give you a kiss,
And a hug!

Spanish Pronunciation

Oy es soo DEE-ah,
Kair-EE-doe pah-PEE-toe.
Kee-ERRO day-SEAR-lay,
Day mee cor-ah-soan-SEE-toe,
Kay yo lay kee-ERRO,
Ee lay ah-DORE-oh.
Lay doy oon BAY-so,
Ee oon ah-BRAH-so!

Fourth of July

Sung to: *Over the River and Through the Woods*

C
El día de independencia,
C   C
Fourth of July.
     Dm   G₇   C Am
Los fuegos artificiales,
D₇   G
Fireworks in the sky.

C
El día de independencia,
F   C
Fourth of July.
F   B₇   C Am
Pasan los desfiles,
C   G₇   C
Parades passing by.

Sonya Kranwinkel

English Translation

Independence Day,
Fourth of July.
The fireworks,
Fireworks in the sky.

Independence Day,
Fourth of July.
The parades pass by,
Parades passing by.

Spanish Pronunciation

El DEE-ah day een-dep-en-DENCE-see-ah,
Fourth of July.
Loace FWAY-goce ar-tee-fee-SHAL-ace,
Fireworks in the sky.

El DEE-ah day een-dep-en-DENCE-see-ah,
Fourth of July.
PA-sahn loace dace-FEE-lace,
Parades passing by.

It's Hot!

Sung to: *The Farmer in the Dell*

F
¡Ay! ¡Qué calor!

¡Ay! ¡Qué calor!

It's hot in the summertime,
C₇   F
¡Ay! ¡Qué calor!
> *(Pretend to wipe sweat from your brow.)*

F
¡Qué fuerte el sol!

¡Qué fuerte el sol!

The sun beats down in summertime,
C₇   F
¡Qué fuerte el sol!
> *(Pretend to shade your eyes.)*

Diane Thom

English Translation	**Spanish Pronunciation**
Wow! It sure is hot!	I! Kay kah-LOAR!
Wow! It sure is hot!	I! Kay kah-LOAR!
It's hot in the summertime,	It's hot in the summertime,
Wow! It sure is hot!	I! Kay kah-LOAR!
The sun sure is strong!	Kay FWERR-tay el sole!
The sun sure is strong!	Kay FWERR-tay el sole!
The sun beats down in summertime,	The sun beats down in summertime,
The sun sure is strong!	Kay FWERR-tay el sole!

Playing in the Sand

Sung to: *He's Got the Whole World in His Hands*

F
Let's play in the sand.

Juguemos en la arena.
C₇
Let's play in the sand.

Juguemos en la arena.

F
Yo cubro tus pies.

I cover up your feet.
C₇
Tu cubres mis pies.
F
And you cover up mine.

F
Let's make a castle out of sand.
C₇
Hagamos un castillo de arena.
F
Let's make a castle out of sand.
C₇   F
Hagamos un castillo de arena.

Sonya Kranwinkel

English Translation

Let's play in the sand.
Let's play in the sand.
Let's play in the sand.
Let's play in the sand.

I cover up your feet.
I cover up your feet.
You cover up my feet.
And you cover up mine.

Let's make a castle out of sand.
Let's make a castle of sand.
Let's make a castle out of sand.
Let's make a castle of sand.

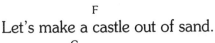

Spanish Pronunciation

Let's play in the sand.
Hoo-GEH-moce en lar-EN-ah.
Let's play in the sand.
Hoo-GEH-moce en lar-EN-ah.

Yo COO-bro toos pee-ES.
I cover up your feet.
Too COO-bress meese pee-ES.
And you cover up mine.

Let's make a castle out of sand.
Ah-GA-moce oon kah-STEE-yo day ar-EN-ah.
Let's make a castle out of sand.
Ah-GA-moce oon kah-STEE-yo day ar-EN-ah.

I Like the Beach

Sung to: *Colonel Boogie March (song from The Bridge Over the River Kwai)*

C
The beach,

Oh, how I like the beach!

La playa,
       G₇
Me gusta la playa.
              C
La arena, el sol, el mar,
       Dm   G₇   C
The sand, the sun, and the sea.

Sonya Kranwinkel

English Translation

The beach,
Oh, how I like the beach!
The beach,
I like the beach.
The sand, the sun, the sea,
The sand, the sun, and the sea.

Spanish Pronunciation

The beach,
Oh, how I like the beach!
La PLY-ya,
May GOO-stah la PLY-ya.
La ar-EN-ah, el sole, el mar,
The sand, the sun, and the sea.

Summer Butterflies

Sung to: *Oh, What a Beautiful Morning*

C   B♭ F
En verano, bajo del sol,
C G_7
Summertime, under the sun.
C   F F#dim
Buscamos las mariposas,
C G_7 C
Butterfly watching is fun.

C   B♭ F
En verano, bajo del sol,
C G_7
Summertime, under the sun.
C   F F#dim
Buscamos las mariposas,
C G_7 C F#dim
Dressed in yellow and black.

Sonya Kranwinkel

English Translation

In summer, under the sun,
Summertime, under the sun.
We look for the butterflies,
Butterfly watching is fun.

In summer, under the sun,
Summertime, under the sun.
We look for the butterflies,
Dressed in yellow and black.

Spanish Pronunciation

En vay-RAW-no, BAW-ho del sole,
Summertime, under the sun.
Boo-SCAW-mows loss mar-ree-PO-sahs,
Butterfly watching is fun.

En vay-RAW-no, BAW-ho del sole,
Summertime, under the sun.
Boo-SCAW-mows loss mar-ree-PO-sahs,
Dressed in yellow and black.

I Love to Sing in Spanish

Sung to: *Did You Ever See a Lassie?*

F   G7   F
Me gusta cantar en español, español,

I love to sing in Spanish,
C7   F
Here I go.
    C7   F
Mi nombre es Allie.
    C7   F
Yo tengo tres años.

I love to sing in Spanish,
C7   F
How about you?

Substitute the names and ages of your children
for *Allie* and *tres.*

cuatro	four	KWA-tro
cinco	five	SEEN-co
seis	six	sace
siete	seven	see-ET-tay

Jolynn Villena

English Translation

I love to sing in Spanish, Spanish,

I love to sing in Spanish,

Here I go.

My name is Allie.

I am three.

I love to sing in Spanish,

How about you?

Spanish Pronunciation

May GOO-stah kawn-TAR en ehs-pahn-
   YOLE, ehs-pahn-YOLE,

I love to sing in Spanish,

Here I go.

Mee NOAM-bray es Allie.

Yo TAIN-go traice AHN-yoce.

I love to sing in Spanish,

How about you?

What Is Your Last Name?

Sung to: *Little White Duck*

F
¿Cuál es tu
C₇
Apellido?

What is your
F
Last name?

¿Cuál es tu
C₇
Apellido?
F
It is Brown.

Point to one of your children and
have him or her substitute his or
her last name for *Brown*.

Sonya Kranwinkel

English Translation

What is your
Last name?
What is your
Last name?
What is your
Last name?
It is Brown.

Spanish Pronunciation

Kwall es too
Ah-pay-YEED-oh?
What is your
Last name?
Kwall es too
Ah-pay-YEED-oh?
It is Brown.

My Family

Sung to: *Frere Jacques*

C
Mother, madre,

Father, padre,

Familia, family.

Brother is hermano,

Sister is hermana,

Familia, family.

Grandma, abuela,

Grandpa, abuelo,

Familia, family.

Uncle is tío,

Aunt is tía,

Familia, family.

New Eton School Staff

English Translation

Mother, mother,
Father, father,
Family, family.
Brother is brother,
Sister is sister,
Family, family.
Grandma, grandma,
Grandpa, grandpa,
Family, family.
Uncle is uncle,
Aunt is aunt,
Family, family.

Spanish Pronunciation

Mother, MAW-dray,
Father, PAW-dray,
Faw-MEE-lee-ya, family.
Brother is air-MAW-no,
Sister is air-MAW-nah,
Faw-MEE-lee-ya, family.
Grandma, ah-BWAY-la,
Grandpa, ah-BWAY-lo,
Faw-MEE-lee-ya, family.
Uncle is TEE-oh,
Aunt is TEE-ah,
Faw-MEE-lee-ya, family.

We're Friends Already

Sung to: *The Bear Went Over the Mountain*

C   F   C
Hoy nos conocimos,
G_7 C
Hoy nos conocimos,
                   F
Hoy nos conocimos,
   C G_7 C
¡Y amigos somos ya!

Sonya Kranwinkel

English Translation	Spanish Pronunciation
Today we met,	Oy noace co-no-SEE-moce,
Today we met,	Oy noace co-no-SEE-moce,
Today we met,	Oy noace co-no-SEE-moce,
And we are friends already!	Ee ah-MEE-goce SO-moce ya!

One Light, One Sun

Sung to: *Michael, Row the Boat Ashore*

C
Una luz, un sol,
             F   C
Alumbrando para todos.
 Em   Dm
Un mundo girando,
  G$_7$ C
Girando para todos.

Sandy Minicozzi

English Translation

One light, one sun,
Shining for everyone.
One world turning,
Turning for everyone.

Spanish Pronunciation

OO-nah luce, oon sole,
Ah-loom-BRON-doe PAW-raw TOE-doce.
Oon MOON-doe hee-RON-doe,
Hee-RON-doe PAW-raw TOE-doce.

We're All Together

Sung to: *Twinkle, Twinkle, Little Star*

C
You wear un sombrero,
F   C
I wear a hat.
G₇   C
You play with un gato,
G₇   C
I play with a cat.
   G₇   C   G₇
Even though we speak different words,
C   G₇ C   G₇
We're all together on this earth.
C
You wear un sombrero,
F   C
I wear a hat.
G₇   C
You play with un gato,
G₇   C
I play with a cat.

Diane Thom

English Translation

You wear a hat,
I wear a hat.
You play with a cat,
I play with a cat.
Even though we speak different words,
We're all together on this earth.
You wear a hat,
I wear a hat.
You play with a cat,
I play with a cat.

Spanish Pronunciation

You wear oon som-BRARE-row,
I wear a hat.
You play with oon GAH-toe,
I play with a cat.
Even though we speak different words,
We're all together on this earth.
You wear oon som-BRARE-row,
I wear a hat.
You play with oon GAH-toe,
I play with a cat.

I Have a Hat

Sung to: *The Bear Went Over the Mountain*

C   F   C
Tengo un sombrero,
> *(Pretend to put on a hat.)*

G7   C
I have a hat.
> *(Pretend to put on a hat.)*

                   F
Tengo un sombrero,
> *(Pretend to put on a hat.)*

C   G7   C
¡Ya me lo quité!
> *(Pretend to take off hat.)*

Additional verses: Tengo un abrigo; Tengo dos guantes; ¡Ya me los quité!

Sonya Kranwinkel

English Translation

I have a hat,
I have a hat,
I have a hat,
Now I just took it off!

Additional verses: I have a coat; I have two gloves; Now I just took them off!

Spanish Pronunciation

TAIN-go oon som-BRARE-row,
I have a hat,
TAIN-go oon som-BRARE-row,
Ya may lo kee-TAY!

Additional verses: TAIN-go oon ah-BREE-go; TAIN-go dose GUAN-tays; Ya may loace kee-TAY!

Please and Thank You

Sung to: *Frere Jacques*

c
Por favor,

Por favor.

If you please,

If you please.

Thank you very much,

Thank you very much.

Muchas gracias,

Muchas gracias.

Sue St. John

Please,
Please.
If you please,
If you please.
Thank you very much,
Thank you very much.
Many thanks,
Many thanks.

Pore fah-VOR,
Pore fah-VOR.
If you please,
If you please.
Thank you very much,
Thank you very much.
MOO-chaws GRAW-see-ahs,
MOO-chaws GRAW-see-ahs.

Wash, Wash

Sung to: *Ten Little Indians*

C
Lava, lava tus manitas,
>   *(Pretend to wash hands.)*

G₇
Lava, lava tu carita.
>   *(Pretend to wash face.)*

C
Lava, lava tus dientitos,
>   *(Pretend to brush teeth.)*

G₇   C
Todas las mañanas.

C
Peina, peina tu cabello,
>   *(Pretend to comb hair.)*

G₇
Ponte, ponte tu ropita.
>   *(Pretend to put on clothes.)*

C
Calza, calza tus zapatos,
>   *(Pretend to put on shoes.)*

G₇   C
Todas las mañanas.

New Eton School Staff

English Translation

Wash, wash your little hands,
Wash, wash your little face.
Brush, brush your little teeth,
Every morning.

Comb, comb your hair,
Put on, put on your little clothes.
Put on, put on your shoes,
Every morning.

Spanish Pronunciation

LA-vah, LA-vah toos mah-NEE-taws,
LA-vah, LA-vah toos cah-REE-tah.
LA-vah, LA-vah toos dee-en-TEE-toce,
TOE-dahs loss mahn-YAHN-naws.

PAY-nah, PAY-nah too kah-BAY-yo,
PONE-tay, PONE-tay too row-PEE-tah.
KALL-saw, KALL-saw toos saw-PAW-toes,
TOE-dahs loss mahn-YAHN-naws.

Goodnight, Moon

Sung to: *Twinkle, Twinkle, Little Star*

C   F   C
Luna, luna, goodnight, moon,
G_7 C G_7 C
Keep on shining up above.
               F   C G_7
Shine your light down on me,
C   F   C G_7
Every night, so I can see.
C   F   C
Luna, luna, goodnight, moon,
G_7 C G_7 C
Keep on shining up above.

Sue St. John

English Translation

Moon, moon, goodnight, moon,
Keep on shining up above.
Shine your light down on me,
Every night, so I can see.
Moon, moon, goodnight, moon,
Keep on shining up above.

Spanish Pronunciation

LOON-naw, LOON-naw, goodnight, moon,
Keep on shining up above.
Shine your light down on me,
Every night, so I can see.
LOON-naw, LOON-naw, goodnight, moon,
Keep on shining up above.

Say Goodnight

Sung to: *Frere Jacques*

C
Buenas noches,

Goodnight.

Stars are bright,

Stars are bright.

Cierra los ojos,

Close your eyes.

Buenas noches,

Say goodnight.

Sue St. John

English Translation

Goodnight,
Goodnight.
Stars are bright,
Stars are bright.
Close your eyes,
Close your eyes.
Goodnight,
Say goodnight.

Spanish Pronunciation

BWAY-nauce NO-chess,
Goodnight.
Stars are bright,
Stars are bright.
Sierra loace OH-hoce,
Close your eyes.
BWAY-nauce NO-chess,
Say goodnight.

I Want to Be a Firefighter

Sung to: *The Oscar Mayer Theme Song*

   F   G
Quiero ser bombero.
   C   F Bb C
Bombero quiero ser.
   F   G
Si yo fuera bombero,
   C   F
¡Con fuego siempre lucharé!

Additional verses:
Profesor/¡Mis alumnos siempre ensenaré!
Policía/¡Con crimen siempre lucharé!
Médico/¡Con enfermedad siempre lucharé!
Enfermera/¡Con enfermedad siempre lucharé!
Dentista/¡Para dientes sanos siempre lucharé!
Cartero/¡Las cartas siempre entregaré!
Veterinario/¡Los animales siempre cuidaré!

Sonya Kranwinkel

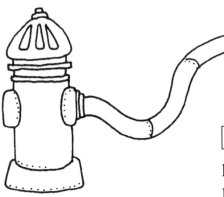

English Translation

I want to be a firefighter.

A firefighter I want to be.

If I were a firefighter,

I'd always fight against fire!

Additional verses:
Teacher/I'd always teach my students!
Police officer/I'd always fight crime!
Doctor/I'd always fight sickness!
Nurse/I'd always fight sickness!
Dentist/I'd always fight for healthy teeth!
Letter carrier/I'd always deliver the letters!
Veterinarian/I'd always take care of animals!

Spanish Pronunciation

Kee-ERRO sair boam-BARE-ro.

Boam-BARE-ro kee-ERRO sair.

See yo FWAY-rah boam-BARE-ro,

Cone FWAY-go see-EMP-ray loo-cha-RAY!

Additional verses:
Pro-fayce-SORE/Mees ah-LOOM-nohs see-EMP-ray
   ehn-sen-ya-RAY
Pole-lee-SEE-ah/Cone KREE-men see-EMP-ray loo-cha-
   RAY
MAY-dee-co/Cone en-fair-may-DAHD see-EMP-ray loo-
   cha-RAY
En-fair-MAIR-row/Cone en-fair-may-DAHD see-EMP-ray
   loo-cha-RAY
Den-TEE-stah/PA-ra dee-EN-tays SAH-nohs see-EMP-
   ray loo-cha-RAY
Car-TARE-ro/Loss car-taws see-EMP-ray ent-ray-gah RAY
Vet-tare-reen-NAW-ree-oh/Lohs ahn-nee-MA-lays see-
   EMP-ray kwee-dar-RAY

I Like to Ride

Sung to: *My Bonnie Lies Over the Ocean*

```
       C        F       C
Me gusta ir en bus,
 C         D7           G
I like to ride the bus.
       C       F            C
Me gusta montar mi triciclo,
 F       G     C
I like to ride my trike.
C           F
Me gusta ir en carro,
G                    C
I like to ride in the car.
C              F
I also like to walk,
G              C
Me gusta caminar.
```

Sonya Kranwinkel

English Translation

I like to ride the bus,
I like to ride the bus.
I like to ride my trike,
I like to ride my trike.
I like to ride in the car,
I like to ride in the car.
I also like to walk,
I like to walk.

Spanish Pronunciation

May GOO-stah ear en boose,
I like to ride the bus.
May GOO-stah mone-TAR mee tree-SEE-klo,
I like to ride my trike.
May GOO-stah ear en CAR-ro,
I like to ride in the car.
I also like to walk,
May GOO-stah kah-meen-NAR.

Let's All Go to the Library

Sung to: *Ten Little Indians*

C
Let's all go to the biblioteca,
G₇
Let's all go to the biblioteca,
C
Let's all go to the biblioteca,
G₇   C
So we can get some books!

Additional verses:
Parque/So we can run and play!
Escuela /So we can learn and draw!
Dentista/So she can check our teeth!
Campo de juego/So we can climb and play!
Casa de Abuela/So we can visit her!
Casa de Abuelo/So we can visit him!
Jardin zoológico/So we can see the animals!
Médico/So she can check our health!
Mercado/So we can buy some food!

Vicki Shannon

English Translation

Let's all go to the library,

Let's all go to the library,

Let's all go to the library,

So we can get some books!

Additional verses:
Park/So we can run and play!
School/So we can learn and draw!
Dentist/So she can check our teeth!
Playground/So we can climb and play!
Grandma's house/So we can visit her!
Grandpa's house/So we can visit him!
Zoo/So we can see the animals!
Doctor/So she can check our health!
Market/So we can buy some food!

Spanish Pronunciation

Let's all go to the bee-blee-oh-TAY-kah,

Let's all go to the bee-blee-oh-TAY-kah,

Let's all go to the bee-blee-oh-TAY-kah,

So we can get some books!

Additional verses:
PAR-kay/So we can run and play!
Es-KUAY-la/So we can learn and draw!
Den-TEE-stah/So she can check our teeth!
CAHM-po day HUAY-go/So we can climb and play!
KAH-sah day ah-BWAY-la/So we can visit her!
KAH-sah day ah-BWAY-lo/So we can visit him!
Har-DEEN so-oh-LO-hee-co/So we can see the animals!
MAY-dee-co/So she can check our health!
Mair-KAH-doe/So we can buy some food!

I Pick Up the Trash

Sung to: *I've Been Working on the Railroad*

G
Recogo la basura,
C   G
I pick up the trash.

Recogo la basura,
    A_7 D_7
And put it in a bag.
             G   C   B
When we go a-walking, I bring a bag.
C   G
Recogo la basura,
      D_7 G
Oh, I pick up the trash!

Sonya Kranwinkel

English Translation	**Spanish Pronunciation**
I pick up the trash,	Ray-CO-ho la vah-SOO-ra,
I pick up the trash.	I pick up the trash.
I pick up the trash,	Ray-CO-ho la vah-SOO-ra,
And put it in a bag.	And put it in a bag.
When we go a-walking, I bring a bag.	When we go a-walking, I bring a bag.
I pick up the trash,	Ray-CO-ho la vah-SOO-ra,
Oh, I pick up the trash!	Oh, I pick up the trash!

Let's Help

Sung to: *Oh, What a Beautiful Morning*

C   B♭   F
Cuidemos el medio ambiente,
    C   G₇
Debemos cuidarlo.
      C   F   F♯dim
The environment needs our help, so
C   G₇   C
Let's do what we can.

Substitute Let's recycle, Let's reuse, Let's clean
up litter, *etc., for* Let's do what we can.

Sonya Kranwinkel

English Translation

Let's take care of the environment,
We must take care of it.
The environment needs our help, so
Let's do what we can.

Spanish Pronunciation

Kwee-DEH-moce el MAY-dee-o am-bee-EN-tay,
Day-BAY-moce kwee-DAR-lo.
The environment needs our help, so
Let's do what we can.

Good Morning

Sung to: *Happy Birthday*

F   C
Buenos días a ti,
            F
Buenos días a ti,
                B♭
Buenos días, Juanito,
      F   C F
Buenos días a ti.

Substitute the names of your children for *Juanito*.

New Eton School Staff

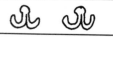

English Translation

Good morning to you,
Good morning to you,
Good morning, Johnny,
Good morning to you.

Spanish Pronunciation

BWAY-noce DEE-ahs ah tee,
BWAY-noce DEE-ahs ah tee,
BWAY-noce DEE-ahs, Hwan-NEE-toe,
BWAY-noce DEE-ahs ah tee.

How Are You?

Sung to: *London Bridge*

C
Buenos días. ¿Cómo estás?
G   C
How are you, how are you?

Buenos días. ¿Cómo estás?
G   C
How are you?

C
Todos listos a empezar,
G   C
To begin, to begin.

Todos listos a empezar
G   C
A fun day.

New Eton School Staff

English Translation

Good morning. How are you?
How are you, how are you?
Good morning. How are you?
How are you?

Everyone is ready to begin,
To begin, to begin.
Everyone is ready to begin
A fun day.

Spanish Pronunciation

BWAY-noce DEE-ahs. COH-mo ayy-STAWS?
How are you, how are you?
BWAY-noce DEE-ahs. COH-mo ayy-STAWS?
How are you?

TOE-doce LEE-stoes ah em-pay-SARR,
To begin, to begin.
TOE-doce LEE-stoes ah em-pay-SARR
A fun day.

Colors

Sung to: *Frere Jacques*

C
Red is rojo,

Green is verde,

Blue, azul,

Negro, black.

Yellow, amarillo,

Purple is morado,

Gray is gris,

Brown, café.

New Eton School Staff

English Translation

Red is red,
Green is green,
Blue, blue,
Black, black.
Yellow, yellow,
Purple is purple,
Gray is gray,
Brown, brown.

Spanish Pronunciation

Red is ROE-ho,
Green is VAIR-day,
Blue, ah-SOOL,
NAY-grow, black.
Yellow, ah-maw-REE-yo,
Purple is morr-AH-doe,
Gray is greese,
Brown, kah-FAY.

Shapes

Sung to: *The Bear Went Over the Mountain*

   C   F   C
Un círculo hoy pintaremos
   G_7 C
Con un dedito en el aire.
                   F
Un círculo hoy pintaremos,
  C G_7 C
Dando la vuelta así.
     (Do actions as song indicates.)

Additional verses: Un triángulo hoy pintaremos;
Un rectángulo hoy pintaremos; Un cuadrado hoy
pintaremos.

New Eton School Staff

English Translation

Today we will draw a circle
In the air with a little finger.
Today we will draw a circle,
Going around like this.

Additional verses: Today we will draw a
triangle; Today we will draw a rectangle;
Today we will draw a square.

Spanish Pronunciation

Oon SEER-coo-low oy peen-ta-RAY-moce
Cone oon day-DEE-toe en el I-ray.
Oon SEER-coo-low oy peen-ta-RAY-moce,
DAHN-doe la VWELL-ta ah-SEE.

Additional verses: Oon tree-AHN-goo-low oy peen-ta-
RAY-moce; Oon reck-TAHN-goo-low oy peen-ta-RAY-
moce; Oon kwa-DRAH-doe oy peen-ta-RAY-moce.

Counting in Spanish

Sung to: *Three Blind Mice*

C   G   C
One, two, three,
     G   C
Uno, dos, tres.
     G₇   C
Four, five, six,
      G₇   C
Cuatro, cinco, seis.
         G   C
Counting in Spanish is fun to do.
        G   C
You sing with me, and I'll sing with you.
        G   C
Siete, ocho, nueve, seven, eight, nine.
C   G C
Ten is diez,
     G C
Ten is diez.

Vicki Shannon

English Translation

One, two, three,
One, two, three.
Four, five, six,
Four, five, six.
Counting in Spanish is fun to do.
You sing with me, and I'll sing with you.
Seven, eight, nine, seven, eight, nine.
Ten is ten,
Ten is ten.

Spanish Pronunciation

One, two, three,
OO-no, doce, traice.
Four, five, six,
KWA-tro, SEEN-co, sace.
Counting in Spanish is fun to do.
You sing with me, and I'll sing with you.
See-ET-tay, OH-cho, NWAY-vay, seven,
  eight, nine.
Ten is Dee-ACE,
Ten is Dee-ACE.

What Time Is It?

Sung to: *Billy Boy*

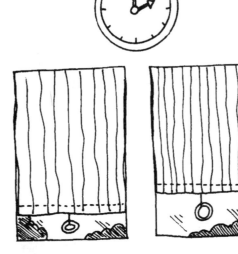

C
¿Qué hora es, Nicolette, Nicolette?

G₇
¿Qué hora es, Nicolette?

¿Es hora de acostarse?
C
¿Es hora de acostarse?

C   G₇   C
¿Qué hora es, Nicolette?

Substitute the names of your children and the different activities of the day for *Nicolette* and *acostarse*.

sing	cantar	cahn-TAR
eat	comer	ko-MAIR
play	jugar	hoo-GAR
paint	pintar	peen-TAR
dance	bailar	by-LAR

Sonya Kranwinkel

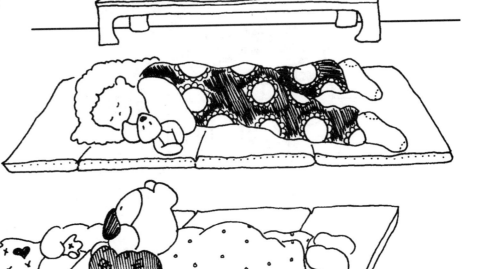

English Translation

What time is it, Nicolette, Nicolette?
What time is it, Nicolette?
Is it time to lie down?
Is it time to lie down?
What time is it, Nicolette?

Spanish Pronunciation

Kay OR-ah es, Nicolette, Nicolette?
Kay OR-ah es, Nicolette?
Es OR-ah day ah-co-STARR-say?
Es OR-ah day ah-co-STARR-say?
Kay OR-ah es, Nicolette?

The Days of the Week

Sung to: *If You're Happy and You Know It*

F   C₇

Cantemos de los días de la semana,

                               F

Cantemos de los días de la semana.

    B♭   F

El domingo, el lunes, el martes, el miércoles,

C₇   F

El jueves y el viernes, y tambien el sábado.

Diane Thom

Let's sing about the days of the week,
Let's sing about the days of the week.
Sunday, Monday, Tuesday, Wednesday,
Thursday and Friday, and Saturday too.

Spanish Pronunciation

Kawn-TEH-moce day loace DEE-ahs day la say-
    MAH-naw,
Kawn-TEH-moce day loace DEE-ahs day la say-
    MAH-naw.
El doe-MEEN-go, el LOON-ness, el MAR-tess,
    el mee-AIR-co-less,
El who-EV-vess ee el vee-AIR-ness, ee tom-bee-
    EN el SAW-ba-doe.

The Months of the Year

Sung to: *Ten Little Indians*

C
Enero, febrero, marzo, y abril,
G₇
Mayo, junio, julio, y agosto,
C
Septiembre, octubre, noviembre, y diciembre,
G₇   C
These are the months of the year.

C
January, February, March, and April,
G₇
May, June, July, and August,
C
September, October, November, and December,
G₇   C
These are the months of the year.

Diane Thom

English Translation

January, February, March, and April,
May, June, July, and August,
September, October, November, and
    December,
These are the months of the year.

January, February, March, and April,
May, June, July, and August,
September, October, November, and
    December,
These are the months of the year.

Spanish Pronunciation

Ayy-NAIR-ro, fev-RARE-oh, MAR-so, ee ah-
    BREEL,
MY-yo, HOO-nee-o, HOO-lee-o, ee ah-GO-stow,
Sep-tee-EM-bray, oak-TOO-bray, no-vee-EM-
    bray, ee dee-see-EM-bray,
These are the months of the year.

January, February, March, and April,
May, June, July, and August,
September, October, November, and December,
These are the months of the year.

Little and Big

Sung to: *Twinkle, Twinkle, Little Star*

C   F   C
Pequeño is little, grande is big.
 G$_7$ C   G$_7$ C
No matter if it's a tree or a twig.
               F   C   G$_7$
Pequeño is little, grande is big.
C   F   C   G$_7$
Great big hog or baby pig.
C   F   C
Pequeño is little, grande is big.
 G$_7$ C   G$_7$ C
No matter if it's a tree or a twig.

Diane Thom

English Translation

Little is little, big is big.

No matter if it's a tree or a twig.

Little is little, big is big.

Great big hog or baby pig.

Little is little, big is big.

No matter if it's a tree or a twig.

Spanish Pronunciation

Pay-CAIN-yo is little, GRAUN-day is big.

No matter if it's a tree or a twig.

Pay-CAIN-yo is little, GRAUN-day is big.

Great big hog or baby pig.

Pay-CAIN-yo is little, GRAUN-day is big.

No matter if it's a tree or a twig.

Goodbye

Sung to: *Clementine*

C
Adiós, adiós,
                          G
Adiós means goodbye.
     F   C
Adiós, adiós,
     G   C
We'll see you next time!

Sue Thomas

English Translation

Goodbye, goodbye,
Goodbye means goodbye.
Goodbye, goodbye,
We'll see you next time!

Spanish Pronunciation

Ah-dee-OHS, ah-dee-OHS,
Ah-dee-OHS means goodbye.
Ah-dee-OHS, ah-dee-OHS,
We'll see you next time!

Animal Names

Sung to: *The Farmer in the Dell*

F
El gato is the cat,

El gato is the cat,

Heigh, ho, the derry-o,
C₇   F
El gato is the cat.

Additional verses: El perro is the dog; La gallina is the chicken; El gallo is the rooster; El caballo is the horse; El pato is the duck; La oveja is the sheep; El cerdo is the pig.

Sonya Kranwinkel

English Translation

The cat is the cat,
The cat is the cat,
Heigh, ho, the derry-o,
The cat is the cat.

Additional verses: The dog is the dog; The chicken is the chicken; The rooster is the rooster; The horse is the horse; The duck is the duck; The sheep is the sheep; The pig is the pig.

Spanish Pronunciation

El GAH-toe is the cat,
El GAH-toe is the cat,
Heigh, ho, the derry-o,
El GAH-toe is the cat.

Additional verses: El pare-oh is the dog; La gah-YEEN-naw is the chicken; El GAH-yo is the rooster; El kah-BY-yo is the horse; El PA-toe is the duck; La oh-BAY-ha is the sheep; El SAIR-doe is the pig.

I Am a Fish

Sung to: *Twinkle, Twinkle, Little Star*

C
Yo soy un pez,
  F   C
I like to swim
G$_7$ C   G$_7$ C
En el lago, el mar, or an aquarium.
         F   C   G$_7$
El agua is my only home,
 C   F   C   G$_7$
I like the waves with bubbly foam.
C
Yo soy un pez,
  F   C
I like to swim
G$_7$ C   G$_7$ C
En el lago, el mar, or an aquarium.

Diane Thom

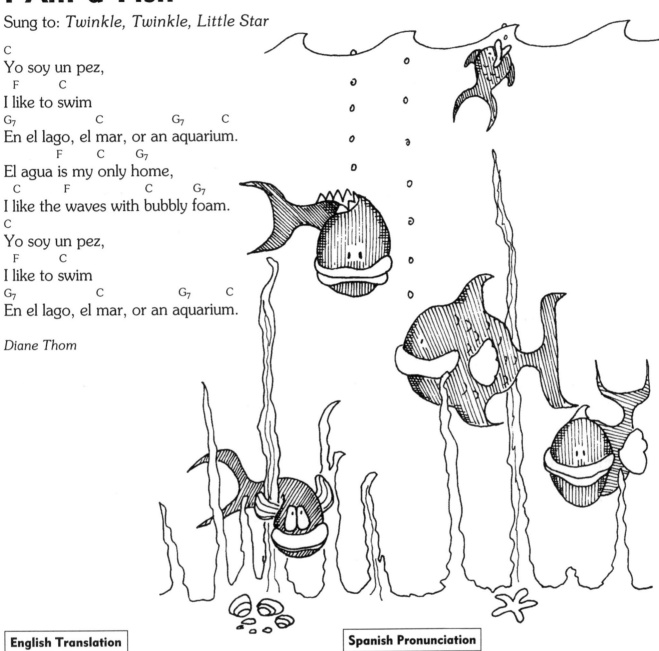

English Translation

I am a fish,

I like to swim

In the lake, the sea, or an aquarium.

The water is my only home,

I like the waves with bubbly foam.

I am a fish,

I like to swim

In the lake, the sea, or an aquarium.

Spanish Pronunciation

Yo soy oon paice,

I like to swim

En el LAW-go, el mar, or an aquarium.

El AH-gwa is my only home,

I like the waves with bubbly foam.

Yo soy oon paice,

I like to swim

En el LAW-go, el mar, or an aquarium.

The Kitten and the Puppy

Sung to: *La Cucaracha*

C   F
El gatito, el gatito
              C
Chases the little mouse.
    (Run in place.)

El gatito, el gatito
              F
Chases him into the house.
    (Freeze.)

C   F
El gatito, el gatito
              C
Chases the little mouse.
    (Run in place.)

El gatito, el gatito
              F
Chases him into his hole.
    (Freeze.)

C   F
El perrito, el perrito
              C
Watches the kitty cat.
    (Look to left, then to right.)

El perrito, el perrito
              F
Simply wants to take a nap.
    (Fall on floor and pretend to sleep.)

Sonya Kranwinkel

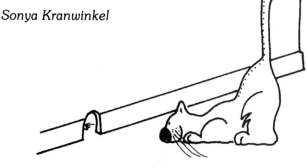

All Around the Barnyard

Sung to: *Pop! Goes the Weasel*

D   A₇   D
All around the barnyard,
           A₇   D
The animals are asleep.
        A₇   D
Duermen los animales,
A₇   D
Sh! Don't make a peep!

D   A₇   D
Here comes the rooster, red and gold,
    A₇   D
Allí viene el gallo,
     A₇   D
Quiquiriquí, he wakes them up,
A₇   D
Cock-a-doodle-doo.

Sonya Kranwinkel

English Translation

All around the barnyard,
The animals are asleep.
The animals are sleeping,
Sh! Don't make a peep!

Here comes the rooster, red and gold,
Here comes the rooster,
Cock-a-doodle-doo, he wakes them up,
Cock-a-doodle-doo.

Spanish Pronunciation

All around the barnyard,
The animals are asleep.
DWAIR-men loace ah-nee-MAHL-ace,
Sh! Don't make a peep!

Here comes the rooster, red and gold,
I vee-EN-nay el GAH-yo,
KEE-kee-ree-KEE, he wakes them up,
Cock-a-doodle-doo.

The Ant and the Elephant

Sung to: *Ten Little Indians*

F
Hormiguita pequeña,
　　(Sing in a high, quiet voice.)
C
Elefante grande.
　　(Sing in a low, loud voice.)
F
Little itty bitty ant
　　(Sing in a high, quiet voice.)
　　C　　　　　F
And huge elephant.
　　(Sing in a low, loud voice.)

F
Hormiguita pequeña,
　　(Sing in a high, quiet voice.)
C
Elefante grande.
　　(Sing in a low, loud voice.)
F
Big steps, little steps, there they go.
　　(Pretend to walk in big or little steps.)
C　　　　　　　　F
See them, there they go.

Sonya Kranwinkel

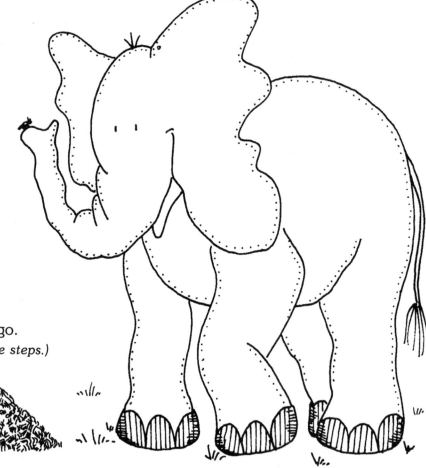

English Translation

Little bitty ant,
Big elephant.
Little itty bitty ant
And huge elephant.

Little bitty ant,
Big elephant.
Big steps, little steps, there they go.
See them, there they go.

Spanish Pronunciation

Or-mee-GHEE-ta pay-CAIN-ya,
El-eh-FAHN-tay GRAUN-day.
Little itty bitty ant
And huge elephant.

Or-mee-GHEE-ta pay-CAIN-ya,
El-eh-FAWN-tay GRAUN-day.
Big steps, little steps, there they go.
See them, there they go.

My Pet

Sung to: *Pop! Goes the Weasel*

    D   A₇   D
Mi perro se llama Fido.
               A₇   D
Mi gato se llama Fuzzy.
              A₇   D
Mi conejo se llama Hopper.
A₇   D
Yo me llamo Sonya.

Substitute the types and names of your children's pets for those in the song, and the names of your children for *Sonya*.

ratón	mouse	rat-TOAN
culebra	snake	koo-LAY-bra
pez	fish	pace
tortuga	turtle	tor-TOO-gaw
caballo	horse	kah-BY-yo
cerdo	pig	SAIR-doe

Sonya Kranwinkel

English Translation

My dog's name is Fido,
My cat's name is Fuzzy.
My rabbit's name is Hopper,
My name is Sonya.

Spanish Pronunciation

Mee PARE-oh say YA-mah Fido,
Mee GAH-toe say YA-mah Fuzzy.
Mee coan-NAY-ho say YA-mah Hopper,
Yo may YA-mo Sonya.

Song Title Index

Totline® Publications

Teacher Books

BEST OF TOTLINE® SERIES
Totline Magazine's best ideas.
Best of Totline
Best of Totline Parent Flyers

BUSY BEES SERIES
Seasonal ideas for twos and threes.
Busy Bees—Fall
Busy Bees—Winter
Busy Bees—Spring
Busy Bees—Summer

CELEBRATIONS SERIES
Early learning through celebrations.
Small World Celebrations
Special Day Celebrations
Great Big Holiday Celebrations
Celebrating Likes and Differences

EXPLORING SERIES
Versatile, hands-on learning.
Exploring Sand
Exploring Water
Exploring Wood

FOUR SEASONS
Active learning through the year.
Four Seasons—Art
Four Seasons—Math
Four Seasons—Movement
Four Seasons—Science

GREAT BIG THEMES SERIES
Giant units designed around a theme.
Space • Zoo • Circus

KINDERSTATION SERIES
Learning centers for learning with language, art, and math.
Calculation Station
Communication Station
Creation Station

LEARNING & CARING ABOUT
Teach children about their world.
Our World • Our Town

MIX & MATCH PATTERNS
Simple patterns to save time!
Animal Patterns
Everyday Patterns
Holiday Patterns
Nature Patterns

1•2•3 SERIES
Open-ended learning.
1•2•3 Art
1•2•3 Blocks
1•2•3 Games
1•2•3 Colors
1•2•3 Puppets
1•2•3 Reading & Writing
1•2•3 Rhymes, Stories & Songs
1•2•3 Math
1•2•3 Science
1•2•3 Shapes

101 TIPS FOR DIRECTORS
Valuable tips for busy directors.
Staff and Parent Self-Esteem
Parent Communication
Health and Safety
Marketing Your Center
Resources for You
   and Your Center
Child Development Training

101 TIPS FOR PRESCHOOL TEACHERS
Creating Theme
   Environments
Encouraging Creativity
Developing Motor Skills
Developing Language Skills
Teaching Basic Concepts
Spicing Up Learning Centers

101 TIPS FOR TODDLER TEACHERS
Classroom Management
Discovery Play
Dramatic Play
Large Motor Play
Small Motor Play
Word Play

1001 SERIES
Super reference books.
1001 Teaching Props
1001 Teaching Tips
1001 Rhymes & Fingerplays

PIGGYBACK® SONG BOOKS
New lyrics sung to the tunes of childhood favorites!
Piggyback Songs
More Piggyback Songs
Piggyback Songs for Infants
   and Toddlers
Holiday Piggyback Songs
Animal Piggyback Songs
Piggyback Songs for School
Piggyback Songs to Sign
Spanish Piggyback Songs
More Piggyback Songs for School

PROBLEM SOLVING SAFARI
Teaching problem solving skills.
Problem Solving—Art
Problem Solving—Blocks
Problem Solving—Dramatic Play
Problem Solving—Manipulatives
Problem Solving—Outdoors
Problem Solving—Science

SNACKS SERIES
Nutrition combines with learning.
Super Snacks • Healthy Snacks
Teaching Snacks • Multicultural Snacks

THEME-A-SAURUS® SERIES
Classroom-tested, instant themes.
Theme-A-Saurus
Theme-A-Saurus II
Toddler Theme-A-Saurus
Alphabet Theme-A-Saurus
Nursery Rhyme Theme-A-Saurus
Storytime Theme-A-Saurus
Multisensory Theme-A-Saurus

TODDLER SERIES
Great for working with 18 mos–3 yrs.
Playtime Props for Toddlers
Toddler Art

Tot-Mobiles
Unique sets of die-cut mobiles for punching out and easy assembly.
Animals & Toys
Beginning Concepts
Four Seasons

Puzzles & Posters

PUZZLES
Kids Celebrate the Alphabet
Kids Celebrate Numbers
African Adventure
Underwater Adventure
Bear Hugs 4-in-1 Puzzle Set
Busy Bees 4-in-1 Puzzle Set

POSTERS
We Work and Play Together
Bear Hugs Health Posters
Busy Bees Area Posters
Reminder Posters

Story Time
Delightful stories with related activity ideas, snacks, and songs.

KIDS CELEBRATE SERIES
Kids Celebrate the Alphabet
Kids Celebrate Numbers

Parent Books

A YEAR OF FUN SERIES
Age-specific books for parenting.
Just for Babies
Just for Ones
Just for Twos
Just for Threes
Just for Fours
Just for Fives

BEGINNING FUN WITH ART
Introduce your child to art fun.
Craft Sticks • Crayons • Felt
Glue • Paint • Paper Shapes
Modeling Dough • Tissue Paper
Scissors • Rubber Stamps
Stickers • Yarn

BEGINNING FUN WITH SCIENCE
Spark your child's interest in science.
Bugs & Butterflies • Plants & Flowers
Magnets • Rainbows & Colors
Sand & Shells • Water & Bubbles

LEARN WITH PIGGYBACK® SONGS BOOKS AND TAPES
Captivating music with age-appropriate themes help children learn.
Songs & Games for Babies
Songs & Games for Toddlers
Songs & Games for Threes
Songs & Games for Fours
Sing a Song of Letters
Sing a Song of Animals
Sing a Song of Colors
Sing a Song of Holidays
Sing a Song of Me
Sing a Song of Nature
Sing a Song of Numbers

LEARN WITH STICKERS
Beginning workbook and first reader with 100-plus stickers.
Balloons • Birds • Bows • Bugs
Butterflies • Buttons • Eggs • Flags
Flowers • Hearts • Leaves • Mittens

LEARNING EVERYWHERE
Discover teaching opportunities everywhere you go.
Teaching House
Teaching Trips
Teaching Town

SEEDS FOR SUCCESS
Ideas to help children develop essential life skills for future success.
Growing Creative Kids
Growing Happy Kids
Growing Responsible Kids
Growing Thinking Kids

TIME TO LEARN
Ideas for hands-on learning.
Colors • Letters • Measuring
Numbers • Science • Shapes
Matching and Sorting • New Words
Cutting and Pasting
Drawing and Writing • Listening
Taking Care of Myself